W9-BXF-047

Energy from fossil fuels keeps cars and other vehicles running on our highways.

Did You Know?
What's Crude About Oil?

The kind of oil found in the ground has several different names. One name is petroleum. The first half of this word comes from the Latin word *petra* ("rock"). The second half comes from the word *oleum* ("oil"). It means oil from rocks.

Oil just as it is pumped from an oil well is known as crude petroleum or **crude oil**. Sometimes, it is just called crude. Crude oil is a mixture of many different substances. Crude oil can burn, but petroleum is most useful when it is refined. The process of refining turns crude oil into separate products. These include gasoline, jet fuel, and **diesel**.

Did You Know?
Millions, Billions, Trillions

Energy is measured in large numbers. For example, the United States uses about 20 *million* barrels of crude oil per day. (A barrel of oil holds 42 gallons, or 159 liters.) U.S. mines produce 1.1 *billion* tons (1 billion metric tons) of coal each year. The U.S. output of natural gas is about 20 trillion cubic feet (more than 566 billion cubic meters) a year. What do these numbers mean?

A million equals one thousand times one thousand. Large cities have populations in the millions. For example, New York City has more than 8 million people. A billion equals one thousand times one million. When you are 32 years old, you will have lived approximately one billion seconds.

A trillion equals one thousand times one billion. Things measured in trillions are very large. For example, the star nearest our Sun is about 25 trillion miles (more than 40 trillion kilometers) away.

"Fossil" comes from a Latin word meaning "dug up." Fossil fuels are found in the ground or below the sea. They are the remains of plants and animals that have been dead a long time. Deposits of coal, oil, and natural gas are still being found, but fossil fuels cannot last forever. People are using them up at a rapid rate. In fact, the people of the world are using them much faster than Earth can make them.

Fossil fuels were formed from the remains of plants and animals that lived in swamps and seas long ago.

How Were Fossil Fuels Formed?

Between 300 million and 400 million years ago, swamps and seas covered the planet. Trees, ferns, and other plants grew in the swamps. Fish and other creatures filled seas and lakes. The seas also held a vast number of very tiny plants and animals called **plankton**. Together, these all added up to a very large amount of living matter.

When these living things died, they began to **decay** (break down). This decaying matter was covered by water and dirt. A heavy, oozy mass of mud and sand pushed down on the dead material. Then, layers of rock formed. They pressed down even harder. As heat and pressure built up, more extreme changes took place. Pressure, heat, and time turned the dead matter into fossil fuels. Plants that lived in swamps became coal. Plankton and other sea life become oil and natural gas. Large pools of oil and gas were trapped by rocks beneath the sea. As a result, the world now gets much of its oil and gas from ocean drilling.

The Demand for Fossil Fuels

The world's hunger for fossil fuels is growing. Each year, more **power plants** are built. More cars fill the roads. More new uses are found for coal and oil. In 1980, the world used 63 million barrels of oil a day. By 2007, demand had risen to 86 million barrels. In the United States, nearly half of the oil became gasoline for cars. Today, the United States uses more oil than any other country—more than 20 million barrels a day. About 40 percent of the oil is produced in the United States. The rest is imported (brought in) from other countries.

Demand for other fossil fuels has also grown. World use of natural gas more than doubled between 1980 and 2007. During the same period, world use of coal jumped by nearly 75 percent.

Did You Know?

Did Coal and Oil Come from Dinosaurs?

For a long time, many people believed that fossil fuels came from dead dinosaurs. Today, scientists know that cannot be true. Fossil fuels began forming more than 300 million years ago. The first dinosaurs did not appear until 75 million years later. Most fossil fuels were buried under mud and rock long before the first dinosaurs showed up.

How Long Will Coal Supplies Last?

How long can we keep using fossil fuels? Let's look first at coal. Using current methods, the world could produce 844 billion metric tons of coal. Right now, about 6.4 billion metric tons are mined each year, so we should have enough coal to last 130 years or more.

This is only an estimate. Many things affect how long

the coal will last. For example, people might find more coal. If that happened, world coal reserves—the amount of coal that experts believe is still available to be mined—would go up. Then, the supply would last longer. Or people might cut the amount of coal they use. This, too, would make supplies last longer. On the other hand, world coal use has been rising year by year. Suppose coal use keeps growing. In that case, the coal supply would be used up much sooner.

Finding More Natural Gas

Predicting how long natural gas will last is more difficult. U.S. government figures say the world has enough gas to last about 60 years. This estimate, however, may be far too low. The government bases its figures on what are called **proved reserves**. Proved reserves count the gas we can produce at current prices using current drilling methods. Gas drilling methods, though, are improving rapidly. New techniques make it easier and

In Their Own Words

"We must ensure that the fuel-efficient cars of tomorrow are built right here in the United States of America. Increasing fuel efficiency in our cars and trucks is one of the most important steps that we can take to break our cycle of dependence on foreign oil."

U.S. President Barack Obama, 2009

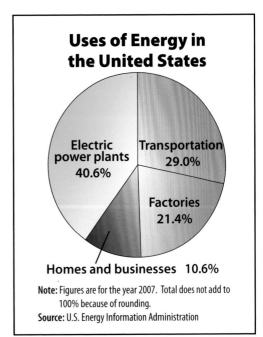

Uses of Energy in the United States

Electric power plants 40.6%

Transportation 29.0%

Factories 21.4%

Homes and businesses 10.6%

Note: Figures are for the year 2007. Total does not add to 100% because of rounding.
Source: U.S. Energy Information Administration

Large platforms are built to drill for oil and natural gas deposits that are found beneath the sea.

cheaper to drill in places where natural gas is trapped by rocks or beneath Arctic ice.

Many experts say that using the newest methods will greatly increase gas reserves. This is very good news. Natural gas is a "cleaner" fuel than coal or oil. This means that it is much kinder to the environment. New drilling methods may allow gas reserves to last as long as coal, or even longer.

Oil—Running Short?

The world is likely to run short of oil before it runs out of coal or natural gas. Transportation in most countries depends on oil.

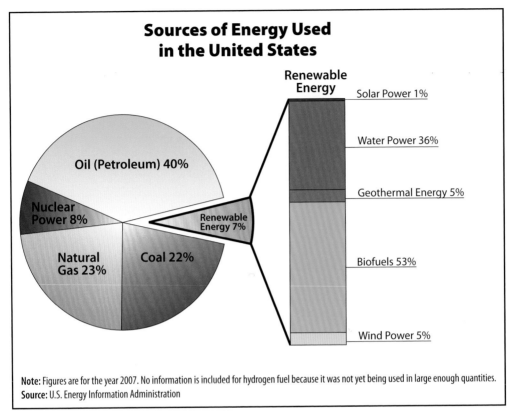

Sources of Energy Used in the United States

Renewable Energy

Solar Power 1%

Water Power 36%

Geothermal Energy 5%

Biofuels 53%

Wind Power 5%

Oil (Petroleum) 40%

Nuclear Power 8%

Renewable Energy 7%

Natural Gas 23%

Coal 22%

Note: Figures are for the year 2007. No information is included for hydrogen fuel because it was not yet being used in large enough quantities.
Source: U.S. Energy Information Administration

How much oil does the world have left? Proved reserves of crude oil total more than 1.3 trillion barrels. That is about 200 barrels of oil for every person on Earth. The supply will not last long. If people keep using oil at their current rate, it could disappear in as little as 40 years. All this *might* happen, but it does not have to. Here are some things people can do to help the oil last longer:

- Continue to search for more oil. If new oil is found, it will increase the amount of proved reserves.

- Improve drilling methods. These will allow people to get more oil out of the amount they already have.

- Build engines that get more power from less oil.

- Replace some of the oil with fuels that will not run out.

CHAPTER 2

The Rise of Fossil Fuels

Humans have been using fossil fuels for a long time. Cave people burned coal to cook food and heat their caves. Later, when Romans came to Britain nearly 2,000 years ago, they were amazed by the jet-black stones they found. Roman soldiers burned coal to warm their forts. Roman metal workers used heat from coal to soften iron. Some Romans even wore chunks of coal as jewelry.

Ancient peoples also found uses for oil and gas. The Chinese burned oil in torches and lamps. So did the ancient Egyptians. In Babylon, builders used sticky **bitumen** (a form of oil) to hold bricks together. For centuries, boat makers applied bitumen to keep boats from leaking.

About 2,500 years ago, the Chinese used natural gas to make salt, which was an important part of their diet. They dug shallow wells where gas was present. Then, they piped the gas to places near the sea. Along the shore, the Chinese filled large pans with seawater. When the gas was burned, it heated the pans, and the water boiled off. Only the salt remained.

Engines of Change

The world's hunger for fossil fuels began with the **Industrial Revolution**. This great period of change started in Britain in the late 1700s. Up to this time, most work was done by hand or with the aid of animals. Most goods were made in small

Smoke and soot poured out of factories that burned coal in Britain in the 1800s.

workshops or at home. This changed with the invention of the steam engine. The steam engine was much more powerful than the strongest person or horse. Steam could drive ships. Steam could pull trains. Steam could power big machines in large factories.

The energy to turn water into steam and power steam engines came from coal. In the early 1800s, Britain mined more than 10 million tons of coal each year. A century later, British coal mines dug more than 300 million tons a year. Soot and smoke from burning coal blanketed Britain's cities.

In the United States, the growth of railroads caused a surge in coal demand. Coal was needed to fuel the trains. It was also needed to make steel

Did You Know?
An Ancient Mystery

Many early peoples marveled at the mystery of natural gas. It was colorless and odorless. People could not smell it or taste it, but they could watch it burn. They could see flames spring up when lightning struck gas that seeped from cracks in the ground. Because of the constant seepage of gas, the flames would burn for a very long time. Early peoples thought of these flames as an **eternal** light. They prayed to the mysterious fires and built temples around them.

for rails. Households began to burn coal for heat. In addition, coal fueled the rapid growth of factories as the nation became industrialized. Late in the nineteenth century, as the use of electricity grew, coal became a mainstay in electric power plants. Many coal-fired power plants are still in use today. The burning coal heats water until it becomes steam. Pressure from the superheated steam pushes against a **turbine** (a rotating shaft) that is connected to an electrical generator. Inside the generator, a magnet spins, producing electricity in nearby metal coils. The electric current that is produced is then sent through wires to houses, businesses, and other buildings.

Growth of the Oil Industry

During the 1800s, the U.S. oil business began to grow. Before the 1850s,

Edwin Drake (at right) dug the first U.S. oil well in Pennsylvania in 1859.

JOHN FITCH

The man who built the first steamboat in the United States was John Fitch, who was born in Connecticut in 1743. Fitch built his first steam-powered boat in 1787. Unlike later steamboats, Fitch's design did not have a large paddle wheel. Instead, the steam on Fitch's boat pushed a rack of paddles that looked like the paddles of a canoe. He built another steamboat in 1790. For a short while, this boat made regular stops on the Delaware River. Fitch also invented a steam locomotive. He died in 1798.

ROBERT FULTON

Robert Fulton was born in Pennsylvania in 1765. He did not invent the steamboat, but he made steamboat travel practical. When Fulton's steamboat, the *Clermont*, first began traveling up and down the Hudson River in New York in 1807, some people laughed. They called it "Fulton's folly." They were wrong. Fulton's steamboat was a great success. By 1812, Fulton was operating steamboat services on six major rivers. He died in 1815. Fulton's efforts helped bring the era of steam—and the era of coal—to the United States.

A print showing Robert Fulton's steamboat, the *Clermont*.

most lamps in the United States used whale oil. When supplies of whale oil ran short, people turned to **kerosene**, which is a fuel made from crude oil. People still use kerosene today in portable stoves, heaters, and lanterns.

At first, kerosene was made from pools and "seeps" of crude oil. (A seep is a place where a liquid or gas escapes to the surface from underground.) Many small seeps were found in western Pennsylvania. In 1859, a retired railroad conductor named Edwin Drake began drilling a well at Titusville, in the same area. His well was 69 feet (21 meters) deep. He struck oil—and a world oil boom began.

The oil industry got a huge boost in the 1880s and 1890s. This is when the automobile was invented. Unlike steam engines, which used coal, car engines ran on fuels from crude oil. Today, most American cars run on gasoline. Trucks and heavy machines use diesel. Diesel packs more energy per gallon than gasoline.

Fossil Fuels Today

Today, about 30 percent of the world supply of crude oil comes from the Middle East. Another 18 percent comes from North America. (This includes the United States, Canada, and Mexico.) Saudi Arabia produces more oil than any other country in the world. Russia is the second leading oil producer, followed by the United States. The United States, China, and Japan are the top consumers of oil in the world.

Oil is produced in two major ways. The first is from wells on land. Since so much oil is found under the ocean floors, the second way is from drilling platforms at sea. Pipelines convey the oil from wells and platforms to oil ports. (A pipeline is a

Did You Know?

How Did Saudi Arabia Get Its Oil?

Saudi Arabia is a kingdom in the Middle East. The country sits on top of more than 260 billion barrels of oil. Saudi oil makes up about one-fifth of the world total. Today, the Saudi **climate** is very hot and dry. More than one-third of the country is dusty desert. So where did all the oil come from?

The answer is that 300 million years ago, water covered much of where Saudi Arabia is now. The oil began forming long before the land took on its present shape. The same is true of other oil-rich areas. In the United States, for example, a great deal of oil is locked in rocks beneath northwestern Colorado. This oil formed at the bottom of a large lake. The lake disappeared a long time ago, but the oil deposits remain.

An oil refinery in Saudi Arabia.

At oil refineries, oil is processed into forms that people use, then carried over long distances via pipelines.

series of pipes, pumps, and valves that can control the flow of oil or gas over a long distance.) From these ports, crude is carried on very large ships called **supertankers**. A supertanker can hold more than 2 million barrels of oil.

Did You Know?
The Oil Sands of Alberta

Canada is a major oil-producing nation. Most of its oil comes from the **oil sands** of Alberta. The oil sands contain more than 170 billion barrels of oil. Only one country in the world has more oil than that—Saudi Arabia. Alberta's oil sands cover about 54,000 square miles (140,000 square kilometers). At least one of every eight barrels of oil used in the United States comes from Alberta.

Sand and clay make up about 85 percent of the oil sands. Another 5 percent is water. The remaining 10 percent is thick, sticky bitumen. To produce oil, bitumen must be separated from the sand, clay, and water. Then, the bitumen must be refined. It takes about two tons of oil sands to make one barrel of oil.

Mining oil sands—
a rich source
of oil—in Alberta.

The World's Top Producers of Coal	RANK	COUNTRY	PRODUCTION (in thousand short tons)
	1	China	2,795,462
	2	United States	1,146,635
	3	India	527,228
	4	Australia	435,690
	5	Russia	345,795

The World's Top Producers of Oil	RANK	COUNTRY	PRODUCTION (in thousand barrels per day)
	1	Saudi Arabia	10,248
	2	Russia	9,874
	3	United States	8,457
	4	Iran	4,034
	5	China	3,912

The World's Top Producers of Natural Gas	RANK	COUNTRY	PRODUCTION (in billion cubic feet)
	1	Russia	23,064
	2	United States	19,089
	3	Canada	6,335
	4	Iran	3,952
	5	Norway	3,270

Note: Figures are for the year 2007.   **Source:** Energy Information Administration

Currently, Russia and the United States are the top producers of natural gas in the world. They are also the main users. Gas is usually carried by pipeline. It can also be cooled and turned into a liquid called **liquefied natural gas** (LNG). LNG is very cold. It has a temperature of −259° Fahrenheit (−162° Celsius). LNG takes up about 1/600th of the space of regular natural gas. That makes it much easier to store and ship than regular natural gas.

China is the world's largest producer and user of coal. Coal supplies about two-thirds of China's energy. The second-leading coal producer and user is the United States. Some coal mines

The World's Top Users of Coal

RANK	COUNTRY	AMOUNT USED (in thousand short tons)
1	China	2,772,799
2	United States	1,127,998
3	India	590,823
4	Germany	281,316
5	Russia	243,960

The World's Top Users of Oil

RANK	COUNTRY	AMOUNT USED (in thousand barrels per day)
1	United States	20,680
2	China	7,565
3	Japan	5,007
4	Russia	2,820
5	India	2,800

The World's Top Users of Natural Gas

RANK	COUNTRY	AMOUNT USED (in billion cubic feet)
1	United States	23,047
2	Russia	16,746
3	Iran	3,948
4	Japan	3,542
5	Germany	3,441

Note: Figures are for the year 2007.   **Source:** Energy Information Administration

are shallow, while others are deep underground. When mined, coal is solid, bulky, and heavy. Most coal is moved from mines by rail or truck. Less often, the coal is mixed with water to form a **slurry**. This slurry can then flow by pipeline.

Fossil fuels are a very big business. In 2007, for example, oil companies had an income of about $1.9 trillion. Five large companies earned about 75 percent of the total. Some of that money was spent looking for new sources of oil. One company—Exxon/Mobil—collected more than $400 billion in 2007. That is more wealth than most countries produce in a year!

CHAPTER 3

Packing a Punch

For many years, the world has depended on coal, oil, and natural gas. There are good reasons for this. For a long while, the supply of fossil fuels seemed almost endless. Riches from coal, oil, and natural gas were like a gift from the past. They were just waiting for someone to dig or pump them out.

The systems that are used to produce and deliver fossil fuels have taken many decades to develop. Billions of dollars have been spent to build them. They are already in place, and they work well. They give fossil fuels a head start over other fuels.

Powerful and Versatile

Fossil fuels hold many advantages. First, these fuels pack a lot of punch. A ton of coal has about 80 percent more energy than a ton of wood chips (which can also be burned). A ton of gasoline packs 65 percent more energy than a ton of coal.

Second, fossil fuels are easy to transport, store, and use. Oil products can be used to run anything from small indoor heaters to jumbo jets. Natural gas is just as versatile. It can heat soup on a kitchen stove or fuel a giant power plant.

Over time, supplies of fossil fuels will run out, but right now, large amounts are still available. China offers a good example. The nation has more than 1.3 billion people. Its population is the world's largest. Industry in China is growing rapidly. So

A worker loads a coal cart in China—the world's top producer of coal.

is the demand for electric power. China has coal reserves of more than 110 billion metric tons. It will depend on this coal to produce electricity. China has already paid a heavy price for its use of coal. Many Chinese cities are polluted from burning coal. In addition, more than 3,000 coal miners in China die in accidents each year.

Keeping Things Running

Of the three main fossil fuels, oil may be the hardest to replace. In many ways, oil makes the world go round. Every second of every day, on average, a plane takes off from one of the world's passenger airports. What powers all these flights? Aviation fuel from crude oil.

In addition, more than 244 million cars, trucks, and buses ride on U.S. roads. What drives more than 99 percent of these vehicles? Gasoline and diesel from crude oil. Where do the drivers get their motor fuel? From more than 160,000 filling stations in the United States alone.

Did You Know?

Products from Fossil Fuels

Coal and oil provide more than energy. They also can be turned into thousands of products. Chemicals from coal and oil are used to make plastics and fabrics. Fertilizers from coal and oil help crops grow.

Oil can be used to make many other products, too. All kinds of plastic products, for example, are made from oil—things like toys, food packages, disposable cups, and the bags you get at the store. Here are some other common items that use materials based on crude oil:

- Bicycle tires
- Paint
- Hand lotion
- Guitar strings
- Tennis rackets
- Trash bags

- Ballpoint pens
- Toothbrushes and toothpaste
- Shampoo
- Surfboards
- Basketballs and footballs
- Toilet seats

Plastic bags are among the many common products that are made from crude oil.

Many buses now run on a type of natural gas, which is cleaner than regular gasoline.

Benefits of Natural Gas

Of all the fossil fuels, natural gas is the cleanest. To cut pollution, some power plants are switching from coal to gas. With a few adjustments, truck engines can burn what is called **compressed natural gas** (CNG) in place of gasoline. CNG is much denser than regular natural gas. It is stored in high-pressure fuel containers. It packs more energy than gasoline and often costs less. It also causes less air pollution.

CNG now powers many public buses. Some school buses also run on CNG. One of the earliest users of CNG trucks is the United Parcel Service, or UPS, which delivers packages around the United States and the world. By 2009, UPS had 800 trucks running on natural gas.

Did You Know?

The Strategic Petroleum Reserve

During 1973 and 1974, some countries in the Middle East stopped selling oil to the United States and other nations. (They were protesting support for Israel on the part of the United States and the other nations during a war Israel was fighting with Egypt and Syria.) Oil prices rose, and supplies dropped. This ban on oil sales was called the Arab oil **embargo**. The U.S. government acted to protect itself against a future embargo. It set up the **Strategic Petroleum Reserve**, or SPR. The SPR is the world's largest emergency supply of crude oil.

The SPR can hold up to 727 million barrels of oil. Four underground caverns (caves) store the oil. These caverns are known as salt domes. They are located in Texas and Louisiana. The SPR protects U.S. oil supplies in wartime. It also helps when disaster strikes. Some oil from the SPR was released in 2005 after Hurricane Katrina hit. Oil from the reserve made up for the oil lost when Katrina wrecked drilling platforms in the Gulf of Mexico.

Energy from Alaska

Alaska is the largest of the 50 states. It is also one of the richest in fossil fuels. Some people think that the United States should make use of the fuel resources in Alaska that have not yet been tapped.

A part of Alaska called the North Slope holds large amounts of oil and gas. In 1977, a pipeline began carrying oil from the North Slope to the port of Valdez, which is free of ice, in southern Alaska. The pipeline cost $8 billion to construct. It is 800 miles (1,287 kilometers) long and crosses three mountain ranges. By 2008, more than 15 billion barrels of oil had passed through the pipeline.

Many animals, including this bird, were covered with oil after a huge 1989 oil spill off the coast of Alaska.

Recently, a plan that would greatly increase production of North Slope gas has been proposed. It calls for a gas pipeline that would stretch 1,700 miles (2,736 kilometers) across Alaska and part of Canada. It would link Alaska with the main Canadian and U.S. pipelines. The plan may also include a branch pipeline to Valdez. There, the gas would be chilled and turned into LNG. The entire plan will take many years to finish. It may cost up to $40 billion or more.

Some people worry that oil and gas development in Alaska may damage the environment. Oil and gas drilling and pipeline building disrupt the wilderness, and oil spills can cause

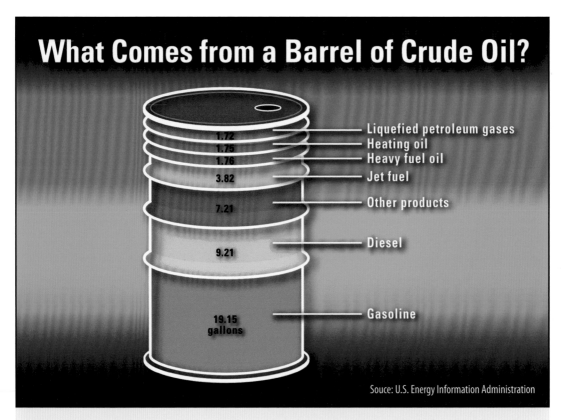

What Comes from a Barrel of Crude Oil?

1.72 — Liquefied petroleum gases
1.75 — Heating oil
1.76 — Heavy fuel oil
3.82 — Jet fuel
7.21 — Other products
9.21 — Diesel
19.15 gallons — Gasoline

Souce: U.S. Energy Information Administration

When refined, a 42-gallon (156-liter) barrel of crude oil yields about 44.7 gallons (169.2 liters) of different oil products.

Did You Know?

The Nose Knows

The main ingredient of natural gas is **methane**. Used in a controlled way, methane is very safe. If it leaks, though, it can cause an explosion and fire. On its own, methane cannot be seen, smelled, or tasted. This poses a problem. How could someone detect a gas leak before it caused serious damage? For safety reasons, gas companies add a chemical named mercaptan. This chemical stinks—it smells like rotten eggs. The foul smell serves as a warning that a gas leak may be near.

pollution problems. For example, a supertanker accident in 1989 spilled 11 million gallons (41.6 million liters) of crude oil off the coast of Alaska. The oil spill damaged more than 1,100 miles (about 1,700 kilometers) of shoreline. Many birds and other wildlife were killed.

For many years, energy companies have wanted to drill in the Arctic National Wildlife Refuge (ANWR). The ANWR is located in northeastern Alaska. It covers 19 million acres (7.7 million hectares) and is home to polar bears, grizzly bears, wolves, caribou, and many other wild animals. Beneath the ANWR lie at least 7 billion barrels of oil. People who support drilling in the ANWR say the United States needs the oil. Opponents of drilling in the area say the threat to the wilderness is too high.

CHAPTER 4

Counting the Costs

It costs about $2 a barrel to pump oil in the desert sands of Saudi Arabia. The price of crude oil may rise much higher when other costs are added. The crude must be pumped, stored, shipped, and refined. All this costs money. In addition, governments tax crude oil and oil products. The taxes raise prices even more.

Pumping oil from a platform in the Gulf of Mexico is more expensive than pumping oil in Saudi Arabia. The cost in the Gulf of Mexico can go up to $25 a barrel. This is very close to the cost to mine a ton of coal in the United States.

When Oil Prices Rise

The price of crude oil may rise much higher when other costs are added. The crude must be pumped, stored, shipped, and refined. All this costs money. In addition, governments tax crude oil and oil products. The taxes raise prices even more.

Oil prices rise when supplies are tight and demand is high. This often happens in the summer. (One reason is that many Americans take long car trips for summer vacation.) It can also happen when wars or natural disasters cut off the flow of oil to countries that need it. When oil prices rise above $100 a barrel, many people are affected. As crude oil prices soar, prices for oil products also go up. Filling a car with gasoline can cost more than $40. Truckers need hundreds of dollars of diesel to fill their

big rigs. Food prices go up, too. When crude oil costs more, fertilizers cost more. It also costs more to run farm equipment.

The United States pays a great deal for oil. In 2008, U.S. companies spent $335 billion to buy oil from other countries. That adds up to more than $1,100 for every man, woman, and child in the United States.

Other Kinds of Costs

Using fossil fuels costs more than dollars. It can also cost lives. Each year, the world loses thousands of people in coal mine accidents. Thousands more suffer from **black lung disease**. Miners get this disease when they breathe in coal dust. Black lung disease makes breathing difficult. Since 1990, black lung disease has been a cause of death for more than 20,000 U.S. miners. The United States has passed laws to improve mine safety, but not all mines obey them.

Some types of coal mining can harm the environment. For example, when coal is close to the surface, a type of mining called strip mining may be done. In strip mining, trees are cut

Strip mining of coal damages the environment by cutting down trees and removing topsoil.

down and topsoil is stripped away. After the coal has been mined, the topsoil is supposed to be put back. Then, the mining company is supposed to replant trees and grass. This does not always happen, however. The result is an ugly scar on the land.

Another type of coal mining is called mountaintop removal. This mining method involves blasting away the tops of mountains (after first removing the topsoil, trees, and shrubs) and vegetation, to get at the

PEOPLE TO KNOW

T. BOONE PICKENS

T. Boone Pickens is a billionaire who lives in Dallas, Texas. He was born in Oklahoma in 1928 and made his fortune in the oil business. "I'm 80 years old and I've been an oilman for almost 60 years," he wrote in July 2008. "I've...found more oil than just about anyone in the industry."

Pickens thinks the United States needs to use less foreign oil. In 2008, he outlined a plan to achieve this goal. His plan calls for running trucks, buses, and cars on natural gas instead of gasoline. The natural gas would be produced in the United States. At the same time, electric power companies that now use natural gas would switch over to wind power. The wind power would also be produced by U.S. companies.

Pickens has discussed his plan with political leaders. He has also explained his plan in TV ads. He has invested his own money in companies that produce natural gas and wind power.

coal below. Nearby streams are clogged with rocks from the blasts. Mountaintop removal can produce a great deal of coal, but it can also pollute streams and turn beautiful peaks into ugly stumps.

Global Climate Change and Fossil Fuels

Global climate change is another serious environmental threat. The climate is changing because Earth is getting warmer. Many scientists state that climate change is causing ice at the North and South Poles to melt. This leads to a rise in sea levels, raising the danger of floods on islands and in coastal areas. If climate change continues, some regions of the world may have terrible storms. Other regions may become deserts. Poor countries and poor people will probably suffer most.

Why is Earth getting warmer? Scientists blame **greenhouse gases**. Some of these gases are naturally found in Earth's

Did You Know?
Air Pollution
from Fossil Fuels

Coal and oil contain many different substances. When coal and oil are burned, some of these substances pollute the air. Air pollution takes many different forms. Soot and smoke can make breathing difficult. Carbon monoxide, a gas that comes from car and truck exhaust, can cause headaches. Pollution from cars, factories, and electric power plants can lead to smog, which can cause lung damage. Scientists are working on ways to reduce the amount of pollution these fuels produce.

Another form of pollution is called **acid rain**. Acid rain is produced when coal containing sulfur is burned. (Oil and coal contain sulfur, which has many uses. For example, it is found in fertilizer.) Acid rain kills fish in lakes and rivers and harms trees. It also eats away the surfaces of paint, metals, and stone. The main cause of acid rain is burning coal in power plants. Power plants can reduce acid rain by burning coal that contains less sulfur. They can also treat coal to reduce the amount of sulfur. An even better approach is to burn natural gas, which has very little sulfur.

Smog, which can cause lung disease, covers the city of Los Angeles.

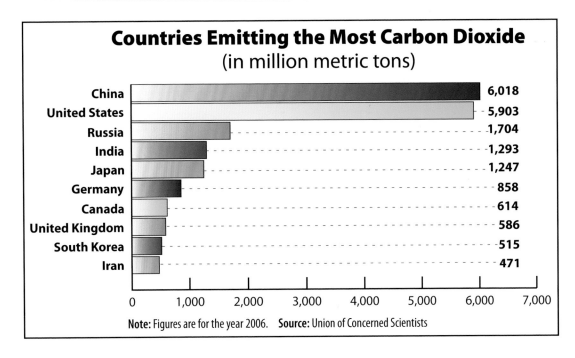

Countries Emitting the Most Carbon Dioxide
(in million metric tons)

Country	million metric tons
China	6,018
United States	5,903
Russia	1,704
India	1,293
Japan	1,247
Germany	858
Canada	614
United Kingdom	586
South Korea	515
Iran	471

Note: Figures are for the year 2006.   Source: Union of Concerned Scientists

atmosphere. When sunlight passes through the atmosphere, some of the Sun's energy is absorbed, and a large amount of it bounces back toward space. There has been a buildup of greenhouse gases in the atmosphere, however, which means that more of the Sun's energy is being trapped. Heat is building up in the atmosphere. One of the main greenhouse gases is **carbon dioxide**. Scientists write the name of this gas as CO_2, which means one part carbon (C) and two parts oxygen (O_2).

Carbon dioxide is created when carbon unites with oxygen. Every time we breathe, we breathe out CO_2. Plants take in CO_2 and produce oxygen. People also make CO_2 when fossil fuels are burned. The more fossil fuels people burn, the more CO_2 they make. This is a major cause of global warming. Each year, burning fossil fuels sends at least 29 billion metric tons of CO_2 into the air. That amount must be reduced, or the effects on climate could be devastating.

35

CHAPTER 5

Fossil Fuels and the Future

Currently, the world relies strongly on coal, oil, and natural gas. This will need to change in the future. Fossil fuels cannot last forever. **Renewable** fuels will be needed to replace them, at least partly. Unlike fossil fuels, renewables do not take millions of years to make. They can be replaced in a short time.

Replacing Fossil Fuels

One renewable that holds great promise is solar energy. Earth constantly gets energy from the Sun. This supply will last as long as the Sun does—billions of years. Wind is another renewable resource. So is energy that comes from ocean tides. Solar, wind, and tidal energy can all be used to make electric power. These energy sources do not directly create greenhouse gases. Unlike fossil fuels, they do not cause global warming.

Some replacements for gasoline are already widely used. One fuel that can replace gasoline is **ethanol**. Ethanol can be made from crops and other materials, such as wood. In the United States, this fuel comes mostly from corn. In Brazil and India, it is made from sugarcane. Many U.S. cars run on a blend of ethanol and gasoline. This may help the nation use less crude oil. Ethanol from corn, however, is not a perfect solution. Corn is needed for food and animal feed, so using too much corn for ethanol can disrupt the food supply. It can also drive up

Corn and other crops can be used to produce ethanol, which can be substituted for gasoline in vehicle engines.

food prices. Scientists are working to make ethanol from grasses. This would not harm the food supply. Another problem with ethanol is that producing and transporting it take a great deal of energy—energy that often comes from fossil fuels.

Saving Oil

Replacing all fossil fuels will take a long time and may not even be possible. There are many practical steps, however, that people can take to use

At this plant in Beulah, North Dakota, coal is changed into a type of fuel that burns more cleanly.

less oil, coal, and natural gas. Currently, we have large supplies of coal and natural gas, but supplies of crude oil are tighter. Could coal and gas products replace some fuels made from crude oil? The answer is yes. Coal and gas are replacing oil as a fuel in many power plants.

Natural gas can replace gasoline and diesel in trucks and buses. Cars that use electric power instead of—or in addition to—gasoline are also being built. **Hybrid** vehicles can run on either electric batteries or gasoline, depending on driving conditions.

Coal can be changed into a liquid that behaves like oil. It can also be changed into a gas that works like natural gas. Coal-based liquid and gas fuels burn more cleanly than coal as it comes from the ground.

Did You Know?

Drilling Sideways

The earliest oil and gas wells drilled straight down through rock. Later, slant drilling was developed. This method drills into the ground at a steep angle. With slant drilling, an oil well rig built on land can pump oil trapped under a nearby lake. In recent years, another drilling method has become common. This method is called horizontal drilling. First, the drill bit heads straight down. Then, it makes a sharp right turn and heads sideways. In 2008, an international company called Maersk Oil said it had drilled the world's longest horizontal well. The drilling took place in Qatar, a country in the Middle East. The well extends for 7.6 miles (12.3 kilometers).

Sideways drilling works well when an oil deposit is long, narrow, and spread out. For this kind of deposit, a single well with a horizontal drill can replace many wells with straight-down drills. Although a horizontal drill costs more than a straight-down drill, the cost is usually worth it. In some places, it can produce four or five times more oil or gas. Building fewer wells also has less impact on the environment.

Different Methods of Drilling

Vertical Well | Horizontal Well | Slant Well

Fighting Climate Change

Another problem the world needs to deal with right now is climate change. According to many scientists, burning fossil fuels causes global warming. How can the world get companies and countries to limit their use of fossil fuels? One approach is an idea called "cap and trade." This plan would apply to all large companies that burn fossil fuels. A cap-and-trade plan rewards companies that do not pollute. It punishes companies that do.

For example, take several power plants in Wyoming, a state that produces nearly 40 percent of all U.S. coal. Suppose the plants all want to burn coal from nearby mines. Each year, the U.S. government would tell the power plants how much carbon dioxide (CO_2) they can release into the air. This is the "cap." You can think of it as a kind of allowance.

Some power plants will run cleanly. They will release less CO_2 than the cap allows. These plants will have some of their allowance left over. Other power plants will not run as cleanly. They will release more CO_2 than the cap allows. To meet the

Did You Know?

Natural Gas from Shale

Shale is a kind of rock that traps oil and gas. For a long time, drillers did not have a good way to get gas out of the shale. Recently, a new way has been found to do this. After a gas well is dug, a powerful stream of water is shot deep into the ground. The high-pressure stream causes many cracks in the shale. The gas then escapes through the cracks and can be collected. Experts believe this new method can greatly increase natural gas supplies.

Did You Know?

Power from "Clean Coal"

In 2005, large energy companies announced a new project. This project was named FutureGen. The companies said they would work with the U.S. Department of Energy to get power from something called "clean coal." The FutureGen plant would be located in Mattoon, Illinois. It would cost about $1.5 billion to design and build.

Here is how scientists think clean coal will work. The Mattoon plant will use coal from nearby mines. First, the coal will be changed into a gas. Then, the gas will be combined with steam. This combination will produce hydrogen and CO_2. Hydrogen is a clean-burning fuel. It will be used to make electric power at the Mattoon site.

Meanwhile, the CO2 will not be allowed to enter the air. Instead, the plant will use a process called carbon capture or **sequestration**. ("Sequestration" means separation or removal.) The plant will pump the CO_2 into storage sites where it will be trapped deep underground. Scientists are also working on other methods to trap CO_2 or reuse it safely.

A drawing of what the FutureGen plant will look like.

41

People can bring reusable cloth bags to the grocery store. This cuts down on the oil that is used to make plastic bags.

cap, dirtier plants will need to buy the leftover allowance from the cleaner plants. This is the "trade." Over time, the government will reduce the total amount of CO_2 that companies are allowed to release. As the government lowers the cap, all companies will need to find ways to run more cleanly.

A cap-and-trade plan has already helped reduce acid rain. Some experts think it can reduce the threat of global warming.

Cutting Demand

Scientists are seeking new ways to produce, conserve, and replace fossil fuels. This is not a job only for experts. Everyone can help. Here are a few ways your family can save energy:

- Drive less. Instead, ride a bike. Also, take public transportation, like buses or trains, whenever you can.

- If your parents must drive to work, suggest that they car pool, sharing rides with other people.

- Obey speed limits when driving. Speeding wastes gasoline. Driving at the speed limit uses less gasoline.

- Stop air leaks around windows and doors. Drafts waste energy used in heating and cooling your home.

- Adjust thermostats a few degrees up or down. This way, you will use less air conditioning in summer and less heat in winter. This is a very good idea especially when everyone is leaving the house or the whole family has gone to sleep.

- Turn off computers and other electronic devices, like television sets and stereos, when they are not in use. This saves electricity.

- Use energy-saving light bulbs (called compact fluorescent light bulbs, or CFLs) instead or regular bulbs. Turn off lights when you are the last one to leave a room.

- Reuse things whenever possible. This cuts down on the energy needed to make new items.

- Recycle paper, plastic, and metal products. This also cuts down on the energy needed to make new things.

- When you go shopping, bring reusable cloth bags to the store instead of having your items packed in plastic bags. Using cloth bags conserves oil, from which many plastic bags are made.

These small steps can really add up. They can help conserve fossil fuels. They can help your family save money. They can help protect our planet.

acid rain: Rain, snow, fog, or mist that contains acid substances and damages the environment.

atmosphere: The envelope of air that surrounds the planet.

bitumen: A very thick, sticky form of crude oil that is found in the oil sands of Alberta, Canada, among other places.

black lung disease: A breathing disorder caused when coal dust gets in a miner's lungs.

carbon dioxide: A gas formed when fossil fuels are burned; also written as CO_2.

climate: The weather and overall conditions in a place as measured over a long period of time.

compressed natural gas (CNG): Natural gas stored in high-pressure containers, which can be used as a fuel in vehicles.

crude oil: Petroleum as it is pumped from the well, before it is refined to make gasoline, jet fuel, and other products.

decay: To break down or rot.

diesel: A fuel made from crude oil that is used in trucks, heavy machinery, and many other types of engines.

embargo: A government order restricting or prohibiting trade and other types of commerce with a specific country.

eternal: Lasting forever.

ethanol: A fuel that can replace gasoline and is made from crops like corn and sugarcane.

fossil fuels: Fuels, such as coal, natural gas, or oil, that were formed underground over millions of years from the remains of prehistoric plants and animals. Such fuels are not renewable.

greenhouse gases: Gases that trap heat from the Sun within the atmosphere; carbon dioxide is one of the most common.

hybrid: A vehicle that has two sources of power. A hybrid car usually has both a gasoline engine and an electric motor.

Industrial Revolution: A period beginning in the late 1700s when factories grew rapidly and steam engines were widely used.

kerosene: A fuel made from crude oil.

liquefied natural gas (LNG): Natural gas after it is cooled to −259° Fahrenheit (−182° Celsius).

methane: A gas used as a fuel that is the main ingredient in natural gas.

oil sands: Deposits containing crude oil in the form of bitumen, along with sand, clay, and water.

plankton: Very tiny life forms that float in the oceans.

power plant: A place for the production of electric power, also sometimes called a "power station."

proved reserves: An estimate of the amount of coal, oil, or natural gas that can be produced at current prices using current drilling methods.

renewable: A resource that never gets used up. Energy sources such as sunlight and wind are renewable; sources such as coal, natural gas, and oil are nonrenewable.

sequestration: Separation or removal. Carbon sequestration is the process in which carbon dioxide is captured and stored so that it does not have to be released into the atmosphere.

slurry: A mixture of coal and water that allows the coal to be moved through a pipeline.

Strategic Petroleum Reserve (SPR): An emergency oil supply set up by the U.S. government and stored in underground caverns in Texas and Louisiana.

supertanker: A very large ship that carries oil across the seas.

turbine: A machine that produces a turning action, which can be used to make electricity. The turning action may be caused by steam, wind, or some other energy source.

Read these books:

Gorman, Jacqueline Laks. *Fossil Fuels*. Pleasantville, New York: Gareth Stevens, 2009.

Morgan, Sally. *The Pros and Cons of Coal, Gas, and Oil*. New York: Rosen Central, 2008.

Raum, Elizabeth. *Fossil Fuels and Biofuels*. Chicago: Heinemann, 2008.

Silverstein, Alvin, Virginia Silverstein, and Laura Silverstein Nunn. *Global Warming* (revised edition). Minneapolis: Twenty-First Century Books, 2009.

Wheeler, Jill C. *Fossil Fuels*. Edina, Minnesota: ABDO Publishing, 2007.

Look up these Web sites:

Adventures in Energy
http://www.adventuresinenergy.org

BrainPOP: Energy
http://www.brainpop.com/science/energy

EIA Energy Kids Page
http://tonto.eia.doe.gov/kids

EPA Climate Change Kids Site
http://www.epa.gov/climatechange/kids

Key Internet search terms:

climate change, coal, energy, fossil fuels, greenhouse gases, natural gas, oil, petroleum

The abbreviation *ill.* stands for illustration, and *ills.* stands for illustrations. Page references to illustrations and maps are in *italic* type.

About the Author

Geoffrey M. Horn has written more than four dozen books for young people and adults, along with hundreds of articles for encyclopedias and other works. He lives in southwestern Virginia, in the foothills of the Blue Ridge Mountains, with his wife and their five cats. He dedicates this book to the forward-looking energy educators of Franklin County, Virginia.